The Greatest Voyages

Published in the UK by Scholastic Education, 2023
Scholastic Distribution Centre, Bosworth Avenue, Tournament Fields, Warwick, CV34 6UQ
Scholastic Ireland, 89E Lagan Road, Dublin Industrial Estate, Glasnevin, Dublin, D11 HP5F

SCHOLASTIC and associated logos are trademarks and/or registered trademarks of Scholastic Inc.
www.scholastic.co.uk
© 2023 Scholastic
1 2 3 4 5 6 7 8 9   3 4 5 6 7 8 9 0 1 2

Printed by Ashford Colour Press
The book is made of materials from well-managed, FSC®-certified forests and other controlled sources.

A CIP catalogue record for this book is available from the British Library.
ISBN 978-0702-32120-7

All rights reserved. This book is sold subject to the condition that it shall not, by way of trade or otherwise, be lent, hired out or otherwise circulated in any form of binding or cover other than that in which it is published. No part of this publication may be reproduced, stored in a retrieval system, or transmitted in any form or by any other means (electronic, mechanical, photocopying, recording or otherwise) without prior written permission of Scholastic.

Every effort has been made to trace copyright holders for the works reproduced in this publication, and the publishers apologise for any inadvertent omissions.

Author
Giles Clare

Editorial team
Rachel Morgan, Vicki Yates, Gemma Smith, Jennie Clifford

Design team
Dipa Mistry, Andrea Lewis, We Are Grace

Illustrations
p8, 15, 17 Fabian Slongo/Advocate Art

Photographs
Cover borchee/iStock
p4 mapodile/iStock
p4, 12, 15 (lightbulb) VectorCookies/iStock
p5 Kersti Lindstrom/Shutterstock
p1, 6 ASKA/iStock
p7 (mountain) DanielPrudek/iStock
p7 (breathing mask) Saulius Damulevicius/Shutterstock
p9, 24 Jacques Dayan/Shutterstock
p10 Stor24/Shutterstock
p11 Viacheslav Lopatin/Shutterstock
p12 Guaxinim/Shutterstock
p3, 13 Maridav/Shutterstock
p14, 24 NASA
p16 Beyond Space/Shutterstock
p18, 24 nice_pictures/Shutterstock
p19 (geese in flight) clarst5/Shutterstock
p19 (geese close up) Wang LiQiang/Shutterstock
p20 longtaildog/Shutterstock
p21 (deer and calf) Mats Lindberg/iStock
p21 (bear) Volodymyr Burdiak/Shutterstock
p22 rooh183/Shutterstock
p23 Imagine Earth Photography/Shutterstock

Help your child to read!

This book practises these letters and letter sounds.
Point and say the sounds with your child:

- eigh (as in 'eight')
- aigh (as in 'straight')
- ey (as in 'they')
- ea (as in 'great')
- ge (as in 'voyage')
- ti (as in 'migration')
- oar (as in 'soar')
- ore (as in 'explore')

Your child may need help to read these common tricky words:

- the
- people
- to
- of
- into
- through
- many
- one
- shoes
- moves
- our
- any
- move
- their
- again

Before reading
- Look at the cover picture and read the title together. Read the back cover blurb to your child.
- Ask your child: *What is another word for a voyage? What is the longest journey you have been on? How long did it take?*
- Talk about the image in the magnifying glass.

During reading
- If your child gets stuck on a word, remind them to sound it out and then blend the sounds to read the word: a-s-t-o-n-i-sh-i-ng, astonishing.
- If they are still stuck, show them how to read the word.
- Enjoy looking at the pictures together. Pause to talk about the information.

After reading
- Talk about the images on page 24. What can your child tell you about them?
- Ask your child: *What does migration mean? Where are the highest and lowest points on Earth? Why do humpback whales migrate?*
- Together, discuss what was the most surprising thing your child found out from reading this book. Ask them to explain why it surprised them.

The Greatest Voyages

People love to explore. We have travelled great distances to discover unknown corners of this world, even exploring beyond Earth!

💡 A voyage is a long trip to somewhere far away.

Animals make astonishing voyages, too. Tiny birds manage to fly halfway around the world each year. Whales swim thousands of kilometres searching for food or warmer waters.

Climb Up

Soaring high into the sky, Mount Everest is the world's tallest mountain. At the top, it is exceptionally cold and there is little oxygen.

The climb to the summit is a huge challenge. It can take eight weeks to complete.

special breathing mask

climbers on a ridge

Deep Down

The lowest point on Earth is under the sea. The trench is deeper than Mount Everest is tall!

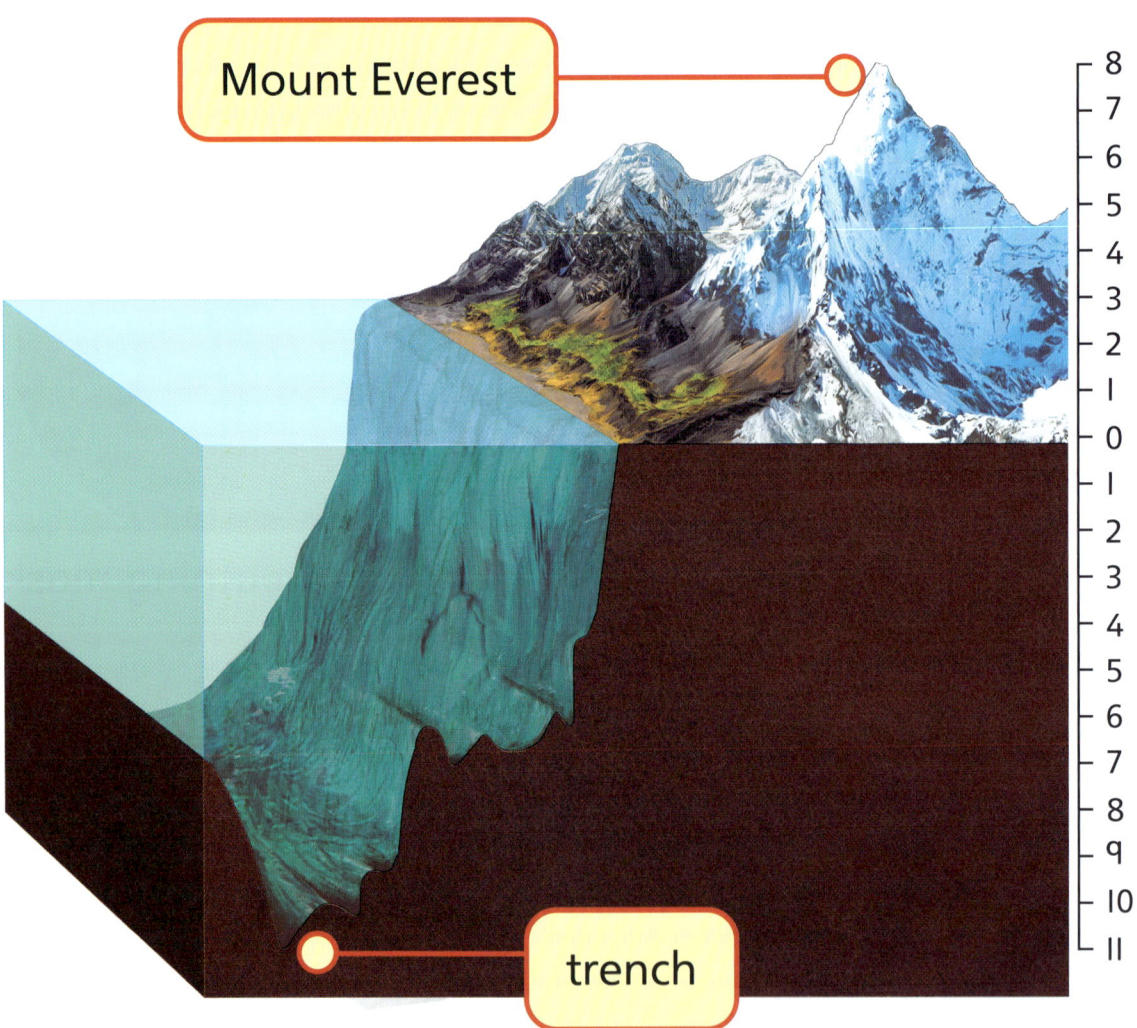

Only a few people on special vessels have reached the bottom.

Underground

Engineers design and bore tunnels through mountains so people can travel quicker by car and train.

tunnel-boring equipment

The longest train tunnel in the world is in Switzerland. High-speed and freight trains travel for 60 kilometres straight under the Alps mountain range.

Round the World

People have flown, sailed, cycled and walked around the world many times.

💡 The largest passenger ship to travel around the world did it in eighty-one days.

The record for running around the world is 621 days. The record-breaker went through 16 pairs of running shoes and came face to face with bears in Canada!

Straight Up

The longest voyage people have made so far is to the Moon. In 1969, a large rocket soared straight up out of Earth's atmosphere, carrying astronauts to the Moon for the first time.

It took eight days to fly to the Moon and back.

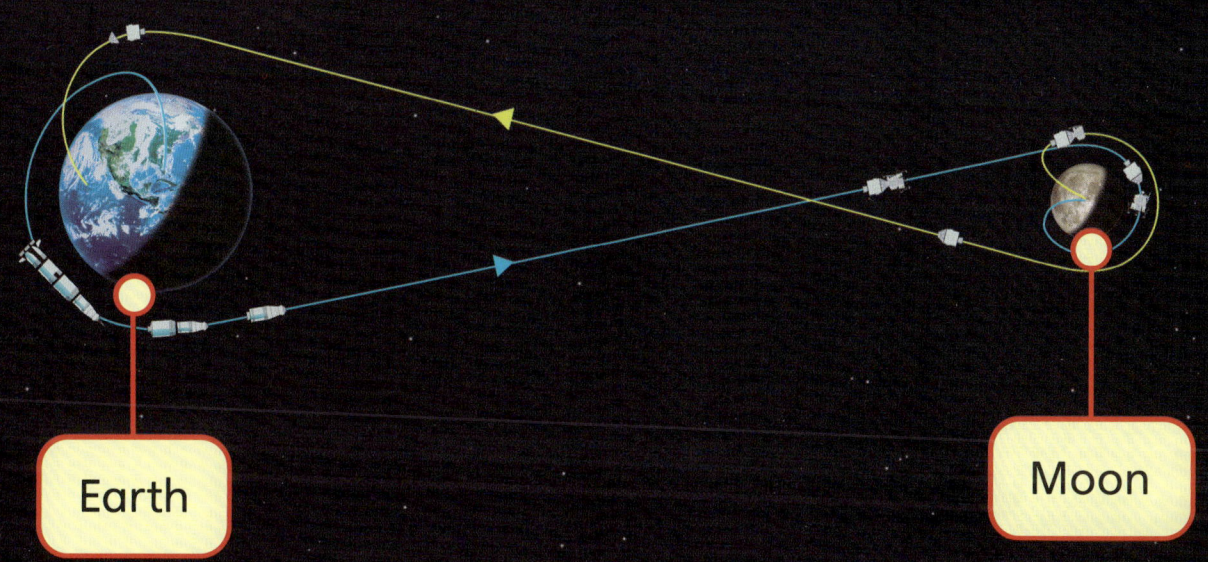

Earth

Moon

💡 The Moon moves around Earth in an oval orbit.

Far Away

Voyager 2 is a space probe. Its mission was to explore our Solar System. It soared past four planets on its course through space.

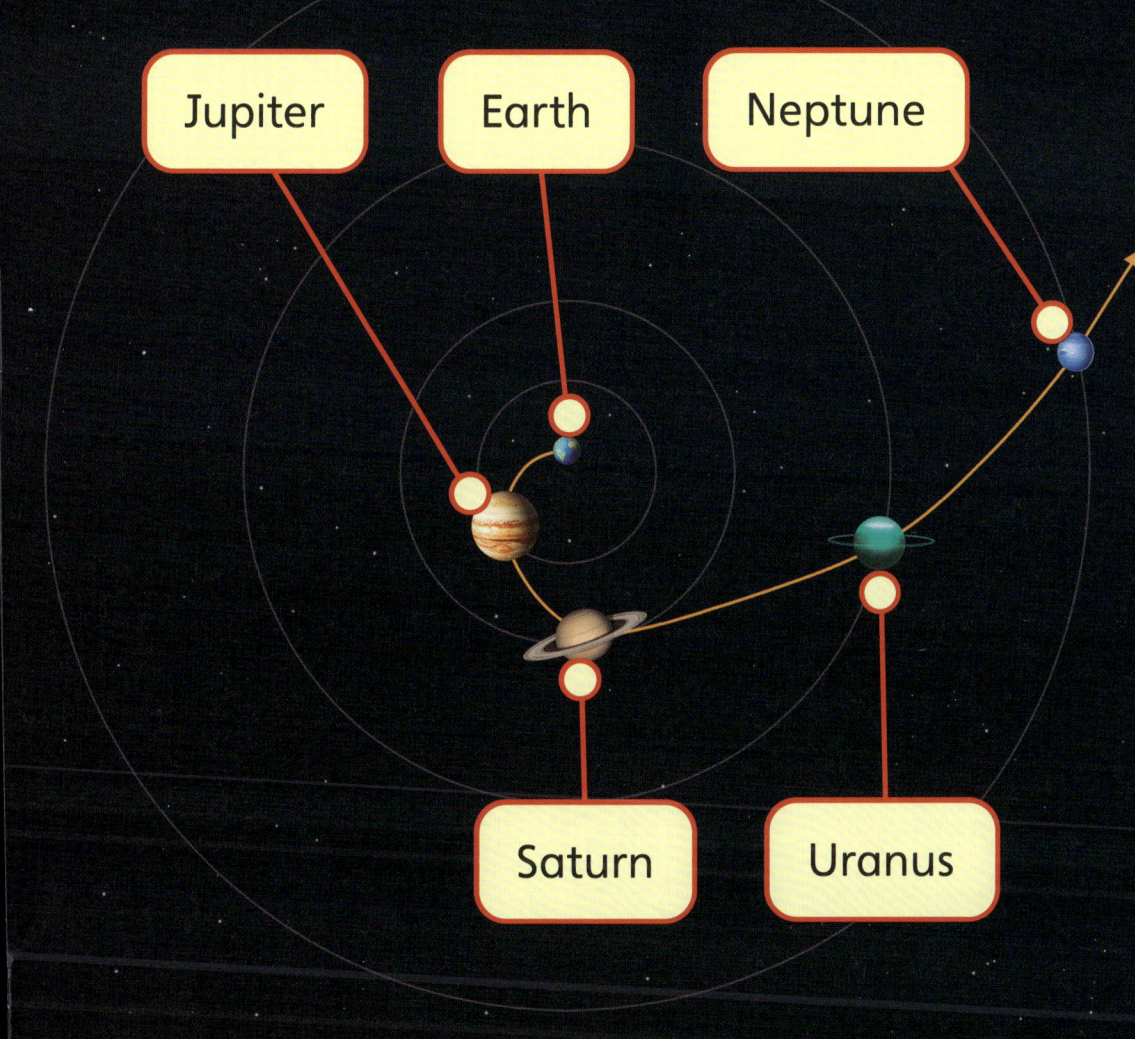

Voyager 2 is now speeding away from the Solar System into deep space. It still sends messages back to Earth.

Great Flights

Many birds migrate. This means they move from place to place for food and warmer weather.

The Arctic tern has the longest migration of any animal.

These geese soar over mountain ranges on their migration. They fly almost as high as Mount Everest!

Long Walks

Some animals migrate across land. In Alaska, huge herds of caribou travel several thousand kilometres each year.

This calf is prey for predators like bears or eagles. Caribou move to places with more food and better shelter where they can protect their babies.

Long Swims

Other migrations take place in water. Humpback whales swim back and forth between where they feed and where they have their babies.

Each summer, humpbacks feed in cold water. Each winter, they swim great distances to warm water to have their babies before swimming straight back again.

Talk about it!